The World of Small

Nature Explorations with a Hand Lens

by Michael Elsohn Ross

Designed and Illustrated by

Cary Michael Trout

YOSEMITE
ASSOCIATION

Yosemite National Park, California

Dedicated to Nick
who helps me see small things.

Printed in Singapore

Bausch and Lomb® is a registered trademark of Bausch and Lomb, Inc.

Library of Congress Cataloging-in-Publication Data.

Ross, Michael Elsohn, 1952-
    The world of small: nature explorations with a hand lens / by
Michael Elsohn Ross; designed and illustrated by Cary Michael Trout.
        p.   cm.
    Summary: Activities for exploring the miniature world of nature
using a hand lens.
    ISBN 0-939666-62-6 (wire-o). --ISBN 0-939666-63-4 (library)
    1. Microscope and microscopy-- Juvenile literature. 2. Nature
study-- Juvenile literature. [1. Microscope and microscopy.
2. Nature study.] I. Trout, Cary Michael, ill. II. Title.
QH278.R67   1992   92-16007
508' .078--dc20   CIP
                                       AC

If you need a new lens or another copy of this book, call or write:
Yosemite Association
P.O. Box 545
Yosemite National Park, CA 95389
Phone: (209) 379-2648

A Guide to the World of Small

Welcome to the World of Small

Welcome to the World of Small! In this miniature realm, a pebble can look like the moon, a dust ball can become a jungle gym, and an old piece of bread can turn into a forest.

Explorers visiting the World of Small usually feel like giants. Be a gentle giant. Handle small beings with care so that you don't harm them. Always return them to their homes. When you explore in a park (national, state or local), look but don't take anything with you.

Are you ready for an expedition? You don't need a compass or a map. Just keep reading this book and you'll enjoy a guided trip through the World of Small.

How to Use Your Lens

Your first trip can be to your own hand. Follow these simple instructions.

1. To open your lens, pull gently on the sides and it will slide out of its case. If it won't come out, you are probably pulling too hard.

2. Close one eye. If you can't, use a finger to keep your eye shut.

3. Hold your lens up in front of your open eye.

4. Look through it. Do you see a blur? You are now nearsighted.

Warning: If you try walking with your hand lens in front of your eye you will be in serious danger of crashing. Also avoid looking at the sun - it can burn your eyeballs.

5. Stand in the light. Hold your lens up to your eye again and place the forefinger from your other hand in front of the lens. Slowly move it back and forth until you find a position where it is in focus.
This is how you focus a hand lens. There are no fancy knobs or rings.

If you don't see your finger, you've probably forgotten one of the instructions like blinking your eye or standing in the light. Try again.

Once you're able to see your finger clearly, try reading the secret message below.

You are now ready to take a trip on a finger tip!

A Fingertip Trip

No Skid Ridges

The pads on your fingertips, palms, and the undersides of your feet are covered with ridges. Just like non-skid shoe soles, these ridges help you get a grip on important things. These ridges are also natural identification marks. Since the patterns of the ridges are different for each person, prints made from the ridges **(fingerprints)** can be useful in identifying people. To avoid detection remember to wear gloves to hide your fingerprints the next time you raid the cookie jar!

Look closely through your lens at the skin on your fingertip. Do you notice all those ridges and grooves? Do you see how the ridges form patterns? Look on the other side of your finger. Compare the patterns there with those of your finger pads. Are they different?

What patterns do you see on your finger pads? You may observe coils, arches or loops. Are your fingertip patterns the same as a friend's? Find a friend and look at his or her finger pads.

BODY PARTS

Skinnytripping

Below are a few recommended side trips to explore other parts of the body.

For the casual observer:

- bushwhack through forests of hair

- follow a wrinkle

- monitor cuts and other owies

- gaze into an eyeball

For the daring explorer:

- peruse a friend's foot (P.U.)

- admire a pimple (gross)

- peer up a nose (really gross)

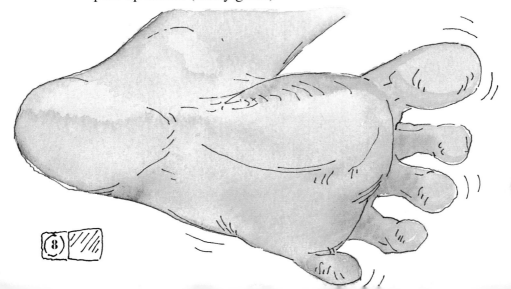

Hair Under Glass

We live in a hairy world. There is hair on plants, hair on bugs, hair on floors, and hair all over people. Each day, animals (including humans) shed hairs and grow new ones.

Use your lens to check out the hairs on your arm. Can you see how the hairs come out of little pits? Are all the hairs the same length? Look for some new hairs popping up.

Each hair is a long shaft of dried cells with a light colored bulb at the base, called the **root**. The root is the living part of the hair and occupies a pocket in your skin, called a **follicle**. When a hair falls out, the follicle in which it was rooted produces a new root which grows another hair. If the follicle dies, no more hair will grow. Baldness is the result of a large number of dead follicles. Ask your dad why all the follicles on his head are dying!

WHAT FOLLICLES?

Give your hair a vigorous brushing. Pull some hairs out of the brush and look at the ends with your lens. Can you find a root? Most of the hairs that fall out when you brush your hair are old dried hairs that break easily. If you want to find a follicle, try yanking a hair out of your arm. Ouch! The whole hair should come out. (You shouldn't need a band-aid for this experiment.)

High Fiber Library

Did you know that libraries are storage sites for dried, mashed fibers? The paper in books is composed of plant or animal fibers which are soaked, mashed into a thin mat, and dried. The finest paper is made from silk or cotton, while most paper is made from wood pulp. When paper is recycled its fibers are used again to make a clean sheet of paper.

Tear a piece of writing paper and look along the edge. Do you notice all the fuzzy, whisker-like fibers? Can you see how they are all connected together in a tangled web? Compare the fibers from different types of paper. Check out some toilet paper, tissue paper or a dollar bill. Can you notice any differences?

Hair You Wear

How would you like to have your hair shaved off to make a jacket for someone? Lucky for us, our hair is not the right texture for making thread or yarn. Sheep, on the other hand, have hair that is both fine and kinky, which makes it perfect for spinning into yarn.

Compare your hair with that of a sheep. Find a wool sweater or jacket and pinch off some of the loose strands. View them with your lens. Are they thicker or thinner than your own hair? Do you notice how the hairs are kinked?

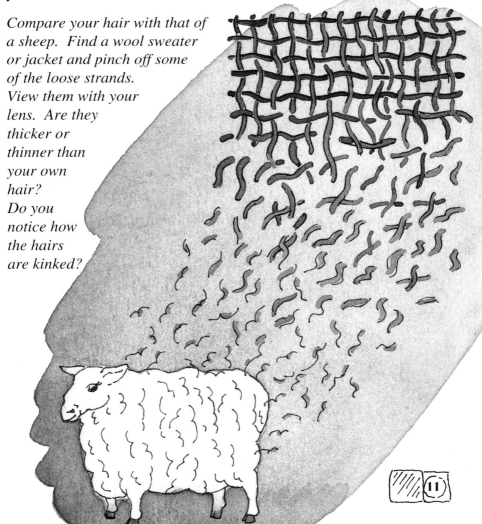

HAIR

Be a Clothes Inspector

Besides wool, clothes are also made of cotton, linen and synthetic fibers. Cotton and linen are plant fibers. Synthetic fibers, such as polyester, lycra, and nylon, come from petroleum.

Rummage through your closet and read the labels on your clothes to find a variety of fibers. Compare the appearances of the different fibers under your lens. Do you notice that polyester fibers shine and that cotton threads are covered with many loose strands? If you study different materials long enough you should be able to identify the type of fabric a piece of clothing is made of without even looking at the label. People will be wondering if you have been rummaging through their drawers.

Elegant Excreta

Silk is the finest of fibers. Unlike hair, it is not grown by a plant or animal. Silk is made from proteins excreted from the organs at the rear ends of insects and spiders. Silk is much finer than hair. It takes 200 strands of silk to make a thread as thick as a human hair. No wonder the finest silk fibers are only one millionth of an inch thick!

Borrow some silk from your local spider web and inspect it with your lens. Is it thinner than a cotton fiber? Take a look at your Mom or Dad's silk tie or shirt (with their permission). Does it look different from the other fabrics?

Fuzzy Forests

Many plants are covered with hairs. Plants have hairy leaves, stems, roots and even flowers. These hairs are found in at least thirty different varieties from the soft furry hairs of begonia leaves, to the sticky hairs on a tomato leaf and the stinging hairs of a nettle. Hairs can be stellate, hispid, villous or even floccose. Say what?

Look at some plants with your lens and imagine you are an ant cruising on the stem and leaf highways of the plant world. What kind of hairy forests do you encounter? Can you find any cozy carpets or dangerous thickets of prickly or noxious hairs?

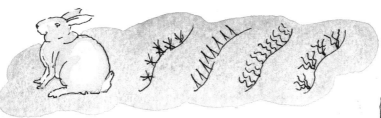

Meet a Drip

Plink...plink...plink. You have probably listened to a dripping faucet before, but have you ever met a drip? If you encountered a water drop in outer space it would look like a ball because there is no gravity. If you want to find out what it looks like on Earth, move your lens to the closest faucet.

Pour a little water into a spoon. Observe the water with your lens as you gently tilt the spoon. Can you see how it stretches to become a hanging teardrop? Watch as it plunges. As it falls you might steal a glimpse of it looking like a silver ball. Catch a drop on a plate or other flat surface. Examine it with your lens and the drop will look like a glinting dome. It is a ball flattened by Earth's gravity.

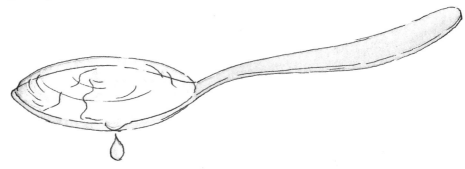

Tickle a Drip

Water doesn't really have skin, but the stretched outer surface of a drop is like a skin. It is so strong that insects, such as water striders, can walk on it. It is also sticky. Once it contacts an object, the water sticks right to it.

Look through the lens as you give the flattened drop a very light tickle with a pin. Can you make a dimple on its "skin?" What happens to the skin of the drop when you place another drop of water on it? Let another drop fall onto the first drop. Now try cutting the newly formed drop in half with a pin. Look at the pin with the lens. Are there water drops on it? Is the water sticky? Can you shake all the water off the pin?

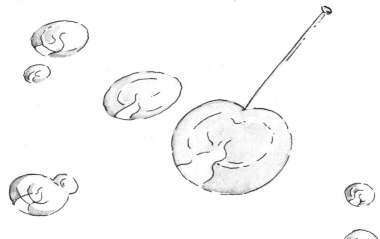

Look Through a Drip

Drip a water drop right here on this page and look at a letter through it.

You are witnessing a special quality of water first noticed thousands of years ago. Way back in ancient times, during the days of the Greek empire, people used water as a magnifier. They made special glass bulbs to hold the water and went around looking at weird stuff like you do. Can you believe that just an ordinary drip inspired the creation of the hand lens!!

Lost Feathers

Have you ever noticed feathers on the ground? Some of these feathers may be discarded flight equipment. Wing and tail feathers become worn out when they brush against leaves or branches or are chafed in the wind. Other damage occurs when feathers are nibbled by small creatures, called bird lice. Instead of repairing this damaged equipment, birds just grow new feathers. This periodic process, called **molting**, enables a bird to keep its flight gear in top shape. Most birds molt twice a year. In their first year of life they may molt up to four times! During a molt the new feathers are supplied with blood until they are fully grown. Then they dry out and remain on the bird until the next molt.

Long feathers with stiff ribs come from the tail or wings of a bird. Find a wing or tail feather and hold it up to the light. Examine its tip with your lens. Does it look frayed and jagged? Check out the base of the feather. You will see the small hole through which blood passed into it as it grew.

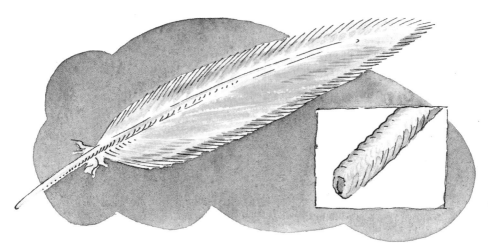

Bird Zippers

A flight feather is like a tree. It has a main trunk (called a **shaft**), branches (called **barbs**) and smaller side branches (called **barbules**). The barbs on a wing or tail feather are locked together by microscopic hooks on the barbules. These feathers are so well locked together that they hold birds aloft on air currents! You can't see these hooks through a hand lens, but you can see how the barbules zip together.

Run your fingers down the barbs of a tail or wing feather so that the barbs separate. Look through your lens. Watch for the separate barbules on each barb. Run your finger back up the feather several times, flattening it out. Notice how the air space between the barbs has disappeared.

Down Under

Have you ever wrapped yourself inside a down coat or vest? Was it cozy? Birds wear down coats, too. In fact, we get down for coats and vests from birds. Underneath a bird's colorful outer plumage is a special fluffy layer of feathers (called **down**) which traps warm air next to the bird's body. The amount of down can change with the seasons. In winter many birds grow extra down feathers to keep them warm. The tiny goldfinch may grow as many as 1,000 extra fluffy feathers for its warm winter coat.

Examine some feathers from a down coat or pillow with your lens. Compare them to wing or tail feathers. Do the barbs zip together like those on a flight feather?

INSECTS

Treasures from the Car Grill

Most people think that cars were devised to transport people from place to place, but scientists know that cars were designed to collect bugs. Unfortunately, many insects meet their end on car grills. But if you're hoping to observe an assortment of insect parts, there's no better place than the front of your favorite automobile.

Peruse your car grill on a buggy day and check out the bounty with your lens. You might find...

Antennae

Insects use sensing devices called **antennae** to feel, smell and sometimes even hear what is going on in the world around them. Antennae help insects locate food and homes, and are used to detect enemies. Too bad for the bugs on your car grill that their antennae didn't help them avoid crashing into your car!

Moths have long beaded radio-like antennae or dramatic curved combs. The antennae of some male moths are so sensitive that they can detect a female from miles away.

Beetles possess simple clubbed or many-fingered antennae attached like side view mirrors. Weevil antennae have elbows.

Flies wear brushy or stubby antennae, while those of fast flying flies are aerodynamic. One fine hair is attached to a streamlined base.

Eyes

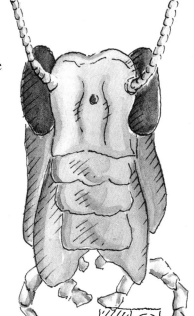

The eyes of movie stars can be captivating, but they are boring compared to horsefly eyes. After all, horseflies have wrap-around rainbow eyes.

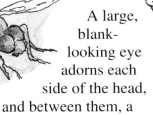

Dragonflies have bulging eyes that can see almost full circle. Bee and wasp eyes look like the headlights on sports cars. Grasshoppers, like many insects, have three eyes.

A large, blank-looking eye adorns each side of the head, and between them, a single, simple eye rests like a ruby on the forehead. The large eyes sense movement, and the simple eye detects light.

More Treasures

Wings

These are some of the more fragile parts found in car grills.

Gently pry some wings off the grill, place them on a sheet of white paper, and investigate them with your lens.

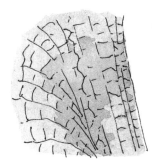

Dragonfly wings look like stained-glass windows. Imagine the veins as the lead parts of the windows. The clear membranes are the glass sections. When an insect develops wings it must pump the wing veins full of blood to make them stretch out. When the wings reach full size, the blood dries, and the hardened blood in the veins provides support for the fragile wing membranes.

Butterfly and moth wings are covered in scales.

Look at some butterfly wings through your lens. The scales will sparkle like sequins. They can be gold, silver, or the colors of the rainbow. If you touch the wings, the scales will come off in your hand.

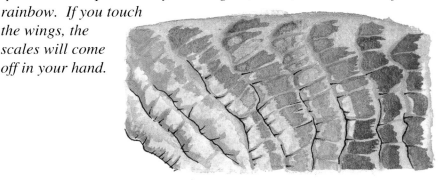

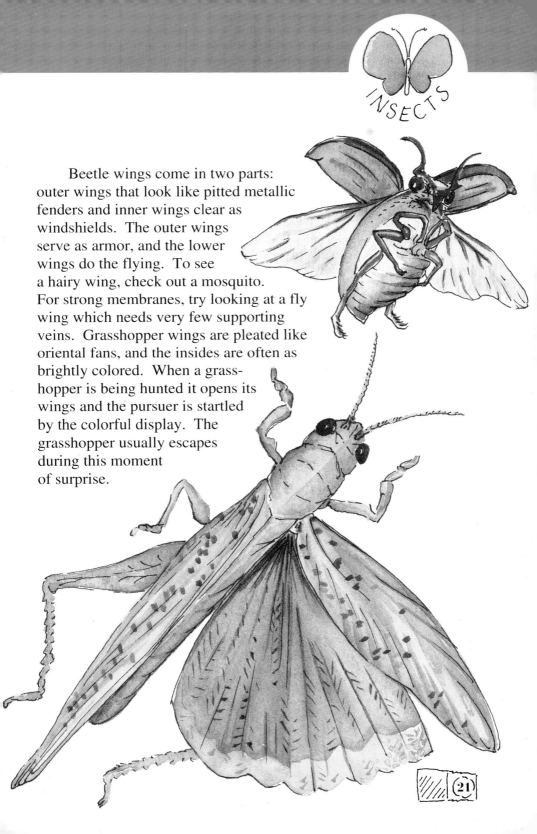

Beetle wings come in two parts: outer wings that look like pitted metallic fenders and inner wings clear as windshields. The outer wings serve as armor, and the lower wings do the flying. To see a hairy wing, check out a mosquito. For strong membranes, try looking at a fly wing which needs very few supporting veins. Grasshopper wings are pleated like oriental fans, and the insides are often as brightly colored. When a grass-hopper is being hunted it opens its wings and the pursuer is startled by the colorful display. The grasshopper usually escapes during this moment of surprise.

21

INSECTS

Mouthparts

Pretend you are an insect dentist. Do you think you would get much business? Peer at some bug mouths. Have your patients say "ahh!"

Insects don't have teeth, but they have other mouth parts well suited for eating their favorite foods. House flies sop up slop with sponge mouths. Mosquitoes and cicadas drink through needles. Beetles and grasshoppers chomp with jagged jaws which are hidden under a flap called the **labium**. Bees and butterflies slurp through straws. A butterfly tongue is coiled when not in use. Pry a coiled tongue open by gently inserting a pine needle or grass stem at its center and slowly pulling outward. You may be surprised at its length.

If it's winter or you live where people don't drive cars, you can still find dead bugs on window sills, especially in messy houses. Another place to find preserved bug specimens is in spider webs.

INSECTS

Life on a Stem

The World of Small is full of big dramas. One of the easiest to tune into is the life on a stem. Stems support plants and also provide their plumbing. Water and minerals flow up stems from the roots. Sugar, called **sap**, flows down from the leaves through stems to all parts of a plant. Maple syrup is sap stolen from a maple tree. The sap is boiled to concentrate its sugars. If you had a sharp pointed straw for a mouth, imagine all the sweet sap you could drink.

Examine the stems of plants, such as roses, and you might find small colonies of animals stealing their sweet sap.

Plant Cows

The aphid is the most abundant of sap stealers. Like slow-moving cows, aphids are easy to watch since they spend most of their lives sucking plants. Aphids don't dance or sing, but they are truly amazing creatures.

Get nosy and peer at the rear of an aphid through your lens. Do you notice small drops of clear fluid coming out its posterior?

This is excess sap that the aphid must get rid of. If aphids didn't release the sap as it came through their bodies, they would eventually become so full that they would explode. These drops of sap which come out of the aphid are called **honeydew**. They are only partially digested and thus, still contain sugar.

Sapmaids

A good way to locate aphids is to find ants. Ants get honeydew from aphids like a milkmaid gets milk from a cow.

Search for ants marching up a stem and then look for aphids. Watch the aphids and see if you can notice how the ants get honeydew.

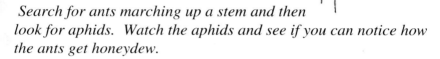

Plant Wolves

As you watch the aphids you might encounter other animals in search of food. Hungry hunters, such as lady bugs and young lacewings, are constantly searching for sweet aphids to munch, like wolves attacking a herd of caribou.

Spy on a stem for awhile and you might be able to witness ladybugs or lacewings catching aphids for dinner. You might also see a tiny black wasp dart into a colony of aphids and sting several of them. This is a female wasp laying eggs. When the wasp eggs hatch inside the aphid, the baby wasps feed on the insides of the aphid which eventually dies. The wasps then spin cocoons and emerge a few weeks later as adults.

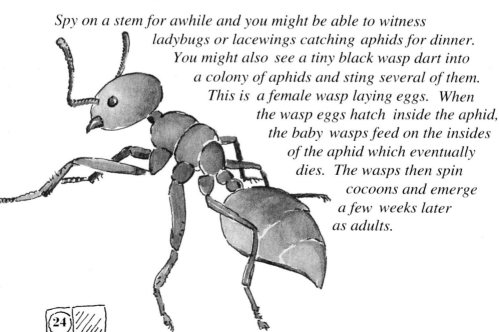

Aphids and More Aphids

The aphids look so slow and helpless. How do they survive?
As you watch, you might notice an aphid giving birth to a live
baby. During the summer aphids are continually giving birth to
live young. While some aphids are eaten, others are born
and the colony survives and grows. Aphids also get
protection from the ants that feed from them.

*Place a ladybug on a
stem with ants and
aphids. Do the
ants chase
the lady-
bug
away?*

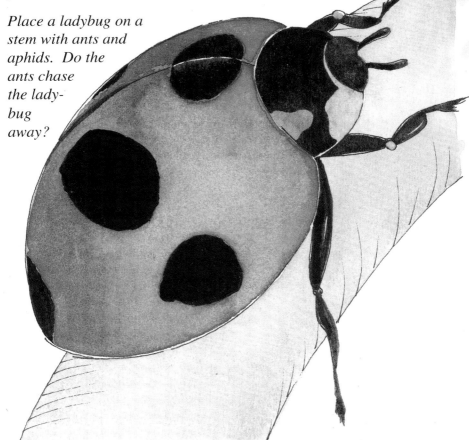

Scales and Spit

Besides aphids, a legion of other inactive creatures sucks sap. Unlike aphids, scale insects protect themselves from attack with a shell-like covering made of wax and old skins. One scale insect produces a type of wax called **lac** which can be melted off the branches and made into lacquer and varnish. Others produce a cotton wax.

Mealy bugs produce honeydew like the aphids do. Sometimes so much honeydew is made by a colony that it solidifies into sweet sugary cakes called **manna**.

Look for scale bugs on the branches of trees and shrubs. Many appear to be part of the plant. Gently scrape them off with your fingernail, and you will see that they possess a head and legs. When you're done, return them to their stem.

Spittlebugs protect themselves in a mass of spit made by combining excess plant sap with a sticky substance, then frothing the mixture up with air.

Search for balls of spittle on the stems of plants in a garden or field. Brush away the spit if you want to see the pale creature inside.

The Big Chill

Imagine it's late at night and you're chewing on your finger-nails as you watch *The Fly That Ate Miami*. The fly is giant, bristly, and disgusting, and you are glued to the screen in fascination. Flies and other small critters are more intriguing when you can see them in detail.

Your hand lens can reveal the beautiful structures and odd behavior of small critters. Butterfly wings look like abstract paintings, and pillbugs look like armored tanks. All you have to do is to get them to stay still long enough. Insects, spiders and other cold-blooded animals slow down as they get chilled.

If you want to examine a live hopping critter like a cricket, all you have to do is cool it off by placing it in a refrigerator. Many insects spend winter in a cooled state and need no food since they are entirely inactive.

Collect a variety of insects and other small creatures (but not in public parks). A good place to find them is under logs or stones. After collecting, roll the rocks and logs back to their original places to prevent animal homes from being destroyed. Put the critters in a container and place them in the refrigerator. Also refrigerate a light-colored plate for later use as a cool examination table. After an hour take your bugs out and place them on the plate. The coolness of the plate will keep these critters still for awhile longer, but they will eventually begin to warm up and move.

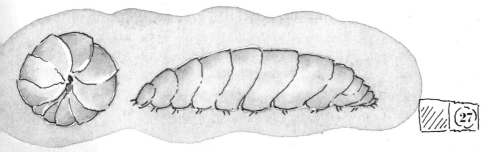

INSECTS

Parts Department

Small animals can be identified by examining their body parts. An insect, such as a cricket, has three main body sections, while a spider has only two.

Millipedes, centipedes and pillbugs have many sections. The number of legs varies, too; insects have six and spiders have eight. Pillbugs have 14 legs, millipedes have two pairs of legs on each section, and centipedes have only one pair per section.

As the bugs lie still in their frigid condition, survey their parts. Count their body segments, legs and other parts such as antennae. Compare the parts of different animals. Check out the patterns and colors. Many bugs that look black to the naked eye are extremely colorful under the lens. Field crickets, for example, have brown and yellow markings.

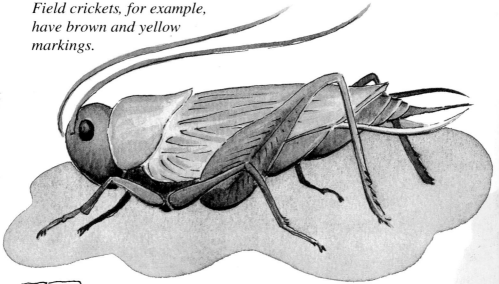

On the Move

As the critters warm up they will start to move, but only slowly. They will need to warm up totally before they can scamper or hop away.

During this "warm up" period watch how your subjects move their legs and other body parts. Do any of them clean their antennae? When many creatures wake up, they automatically clean their antennae by combing them with special spines on their legs. Clean antennae are needed to tune in to danger and food.

Note: Once your bugs start cruising, reward them for their modeling job by returning them to their homes.

Bugs Under the Skylight

It's a good idea to use a viewing container for insects that move around a lot. The clear plastic box in which your hand lens was packaged is perfect for the job. Or find a little box small enough that your hand lens completely covers the top. Put a little creature inside and watch it roam. It's a great way to view lots of other natural objects, too.

Pickles, Meteorites and Sea Urchins

What can be as big as a softball or as small as a grain of salt? What can look like a pickle, a meteorite, a snail or a sea urchin? What can smell like licorice or mustard, peanut butter or celery?

If you guessed a seed, you're right. Seeds are the children of flowers, and they are found almost everywhere.

Go find some seeds. Extract them from fruits or vegetables. Some seeds, such as anise or caraway, are stored on your spice rack. Others, such as beans or rice, are in the kitchen cupboard. Search for seeds on plants in a garden or vacant lot. (Remember not to collect them in public parks.) Place what you've collected on a sheet of paper and use your lens to discover what the seeds look like up close.

Dimples and Wrinkles

Babies aren't the only ones with dimples, and old folks aren't the only ones with wrinkles. As you peer at seeds with your lens you will notice that they have different textures. Some, such as beans or tomato seeds, have dimpled skins, while others, peas and orange seeds for example, are wrinkled. Certain seeds like rice and dill are covered with ridges. Why do you think seeds are so wrinkled, dimpled and ridged?

Assemble a variety of seeds and place one of each type in a glass of water to soak overnight. Remove the seeds from the water the next day and line up each one next to a dry seed of the same type. Can you see how the seeds swelled with water? Most seeds need water to sprout. The ridges, wrinkles and dimples allow seeds to expand without bursting when they get a soaking.

WATER — SWOLLEN PEA

DRIED PEA

SEEDS

Seeds on the Move

Seeds don't have legs, but they get around okay. When you compare a variety of seeds you will discover that they are shaped quite differently.

Each seed is designed for a different type of travel. Some fly, some hitchhike, some roll, and others float.

Parachutes and Helicopters

Many plants send their seeds off to distant places by letting them float in the wind. Down-covered willow seeds float on summer breezes. Maple and pine seeds spiral down from high branches and land hundreds of feet from their parent trees.

Look for a white, fluffy dandelion in the yard. Pull it apart and investigate the seeds with your lens. Do you notice how each seed is attached to a shaft with an inverted parachute on top? Place a seed on your hand and blow on it. Does it float like a parachute? Trim some of the parachute with scissors to discover how much of it is needed for the seed to float in the air.

*If you have any maple trees nearby, look for the maple **samaras**. They look like one airplane wing with a seed attached. Use your lens to look at a samara from the side. Does it look streamlined like an airplane wing? Stand on a chair and drop the samara. How does it fly?*

Walk a Seed

Have you ever found a seed attached to your shoelaces or socks? Have you ever wondered how it got there? Many seeds have hooks which latch onto the fur (or clothes) of any animal that brushes up against them. The seeds then ride to wherever the animal finally grooms itself and picks off the sticky hitchhikers.

Take a walk through a field when the grass and flowers are dry, then check your socks. With your lens examine any seeds that you find. Do any look like a harpoon? Some seeds have a spurred point attached to a long shaft. When one lodges in your sock, the spur prevents the seed from coming out. The only way to remove the seed is to push it all the way through your sock. Do you notice any with hooks? If you have shoes or a jacket with Velcro closures, compare the hooks on a burr to the stiff side of the Velcro closure. It's no wonder that the inventor of Velcro got the idea from some clingy seeds.

SEEDS

Slimy Journey

Inside wild berries and other fruits are seeds. When a berry is eaten by a bird or other animal, the seeds get a slimy ride. They slide down the throat, plunge into the stomach, and are pushed through the intestines. The seeds leave by the back door, encased in fresh animal droppings. The ride may seem disgusting to you, but what better place could a seed land than in fresh, moist fertilizer? Eat a berry and give a seed a ride!

Compare the shapes of seeds from a tomato, apple, blackberry or orange. Do you notice how they are stream-lined like a kayak so they can speed through the wild rapids of the digestive system?

Little Sprout

Each seed is a package of life. Inside a seed is a small plant, called an **embryo**. When a seed is soaked, it breaks open and the embryo develops into a sprout. Sprouts have a small root and one or two leaves. Spiny cacti, gigantic redwoods and carrots all grow from little sprouts.

*Check out some sprouts with your lens. You can find them in the garden or maybe in your salad. Can you see the seed leaves (**cotyledon**), the root or the old seed coat?*

Sprout Some Sprouts

You can make your own sprouts by soaking seeds overnight in a plastic sandwich bag full of water.

The next morning poke holes in one corner of your bag with a fork. After the water drains place the bag in a cupboard or other dark place. Rinse the seeds each day and watch them grow! On the fifth day leave the sprouts out, and the new leaves will turn green. Use your lens to examine how the sprouts change. If you sprout alfalfa seeds or bean seeds, you can eat them when you are finished.

CRYSTALS

Crystal Clear

Have you ever eaten a crystal? Are you sure? A **crystal** is a solid substance with a number of flat surfaces arranged in a pattern.

Sprinkle some salt and pepper on a sheet of white paper. What do you see through your lens? Do the salt and pepper grains look the same? Scan the grains of salt and pepper carefully. Can you find any that look like little glass cubes or beads? As you can see, all the pepper grains are different sizes and shapes, while the salt grains are more uniform. Salt grains are crystals.

Salt crystals are cubes. Most of them have worn corners from rubbing against each other in the shaker. Do you think that salt is the only crystal that you eat?

Pour some white sugar onto the paper. Examine it with your lens. Does it have flat surfaces in a regular pattern? Does it look similar to the salt crystals?

Crystals Under Your Feet

Another common crystal is **quartz**. A familiar quartz crystal is found in sand. Like salt, sand crystals are rounded by wear. Larger quartz crystals are often sold in jewelry or gem stores. They exhibit the true shape of the quartz crystal, a six-sided shape, called a **hexagon**.

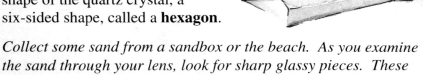

Collect some sand from a sandbox or the beach. As you examine the sand through your lens, look for sharp glassy pieces. These are quartz crystals.

Crystals Over Head

The most spectacular crystal of all falls from the sky. You have probably cut snowflakes out of paper, but have you ever looked at a real snowflake up close? If you live where it snows, try to find a single snowflake. You will notice that, like the quartz crystal, it is six-sided.

The next time you are in a snowstorm, flip out your hand lens and take a cool trip. View the snowflakes that land on your gloves or sleeves.

Be careful not to blow warm air onto the lens or the snowflake because it will fog the lens or melt the flake. Check to see if you are looking at a single snowflake or at a cluster. Can you find any two flakes that look the same?

How to Make Fresh Crystals

Drop a pinch of salt crystals into a bottle cap full of warm water.

Stir until all the grains are dissolved.

Pour a few drops of the water onto a dish. Discard the rest.

Leave the dish out until all the water has evaporated.
(This might take a whole day.)

Look on the plate for salt crystals with your lens. Compare them with some crystals from the salt shaker. Are they different? How? Try the same process with some white sugar.

A Ball of Dust

Dust is everywhere. Peek behind a dresser or under the bed and you may find it in abundance. It begins to appear almost immediately after cleaning day and continues to grow like a billowing storm cloud until it is sucked up in a vacuum or swept away by a broom. What is it made of? Where does it all come from?

The framework of a dustball is made of fibers that you and the other people in your house shed from your bodies and clothes. Other fibers come from spider webs, cloth or pet fur. Hairs are the largest fibers. Once these fibers entangle they become a trap for tiny bits of soil, fungal spores (from mushrooms and molds), ash (from fires), and other small items. Over 43 thousand tons of dust blanket the U.S.A. each year, some of it from as far away as outer space. Maybe part of the dustball in your house is from another planet!

Build up your courage. Snag a ball of dust from under the bed or behind the refrigerator. Examine it through your lens. Look at the fibers carefully. Can you identify one of your own hairs? If you have pets, can you find their fur? Are there threads that match a sweater or somebody's underpants? Look for other items trapped in the fibers. Do you think you might find creatures from another galaxy?

DIRT

A Handful of Dirt

What will you find in a handful of dirt? "Not much" you say? Take a look. Scoop a handful of rich soil from under a tree or out of a well-tended garden. Place the soil on a sheet of white paper and move your lens over it like a low flying aircraft. Here are some of the things that you might see through your lens.

Gold!

Most of the gold-colored flakes you'll find in dirt are mica, a common mineral found in rocks.

Find a gold-colored flake and poke it with a needle. If it breaks it's mica; if it bends, you've struck it rich!

Tiny Chunks of Glass

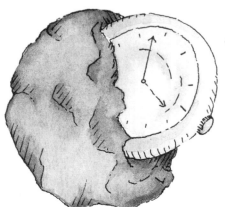

The soil is full of clear quartz crystals that look like glass. In fact, glass is made from quartz. Quartz crystals are also found in watches, but the crystals in soil come from broken rocks.

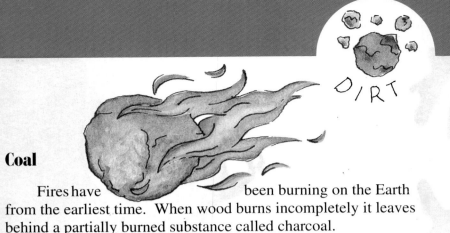

Coal

Fires have been burning on the Earth from the earliest time. When wood burns incompletely it leaves behind a partially burned substance called charcoal.

Try to crush any small, coal-black particles that you find. Charcoal breaks easily. Are there signs of fire in your soil?

Hairs

Yuck, how did the dirt get so hairy? Plants search the soil for water and nutrients through a maze of underground tentacles called **roots**. In just three months a single grass plant can grow up to 7,000 miles of roots and root hairs. That must keep the root barber very busy!

Survey the soil with your lens. How many miles of root hair can you find?

White Hairs

Are white hairs from wise old plants? Those that you find in soil are usually flattened and matted. Unlike roots, these hairs, called **mycelia**, can eat things in the dirt. They are the part of fungi that gets food. In a spoonful of topsoil there may be up to two miles of mycelia busily digesting leftovers.

Use your lens to compare roots and mycelia.

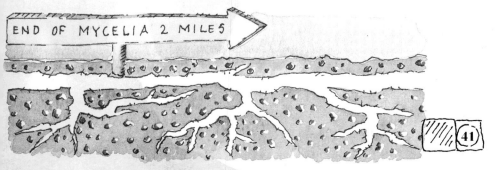

END OF MYCELIA 2 MILES

DIRT

Seeds and Sprouts

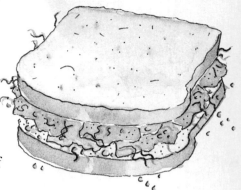

How is the soil like a health food sandwich? (It's full of seeds and sprouts.) Seeds are constantly sprouting in the soil. Only a few make it to adulthood because they are a favorite food of soil animals and fungi.

You may have several different kinds of sprouts in your soil. With your lens see how many kinds you can find.

Fill a paper cup with soil, and water it regularly (enough to keep it damp, but not soggy). If there are seeds in the soil, you'll see some sprouts within a week!

Dirt Clods

Soil is composed of different-sized particles of minerals and the bits and pieces of dead plants and animals. Sand is the largest mineral particle considered to be soil, and clay is the smallest. If a sand grain were as big as this page, a clay particle would be the size of the period at the end of this sentence.

Crumble a dry clod over a sheet of white paper. Carefully spread the particles and view them through your lens to see if you can find

different sizes. If you want to separate the smaller particles, roll some dirt into a ball. Look at your fingers through your lens. The small particles stuck to your skin are clay and silt.

DIRT

Creatures of the Deep

The soil teems with animal life. These are some of the creatures you might meet.

Mighty Mites

Mites are the most numerous land animals on earth. There can be as many as 1/4 million in one backyard. Some are red, others brown, and there are even see-through models. When mites are young they have only 6 legs, then get another pair when they are full grown, like their cousins, the spiders.

Look for these minute creatures cruising, like tanks, in and out of little clumps of soil particles.

Springing Springtails

Hopping and bopping through the soil is the champion of midget jumpers, the springtail. Using a small tail that works like a spring, a springtail can propel itself a distance 40 times its body length (the equivalent of you jumping over 150 feet!). Springtails are almost as numerous as mites. As many as 250,000 can reside in one acre of flipping, flopping meadow.

If you find a springtail, poke it with a blade of grass and watch it spring into action.

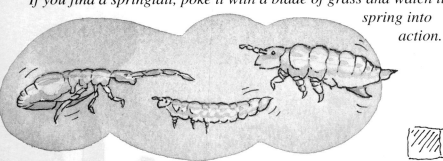

Double Tails or Diplurans

You can tell that these creatures live underground because they are so white. Colors aren't visible in the dark, so there is no advantage to having colorful skin. Diplurans may not look fierce, but some are hungry hunters.

Examine the diplurans with a lens to see if you can locate the pincers they use to catch and hold prey.

Cocoons and Pupal Cases

Soil is a mild and pleasant retreat, an underground Tahiti. It is a safe and cozy place to lay eggs or sit out the winter as an insect **larva** or **pupa** (cocoon). In the spring when the air above ground warms up, eggs hatch and adults emerge leaving behind shells, cocoons and cases.

Examine the surface of a pupa or cocoon through the lens. Can you see through the skin of the pupa? Can you tell what the cocoon is made of?

Everybody's Graveyard

Pieces of all the plants and animals that live in or on the soil eventually become part of it.

Pretend you are a paleontologist (a digger-upper of fossils, bones and other artifacts). What signs of past life can you find with your lens?

Living Diapers

Do you remember when you wore diapers? Did your mother and father get them from a tree? If you were a baby back in the old, old days when most people shopped in the fields and forests, you might have worn diapers made of moss. **Moss** is a plant without roots that sucks up water like a sponge. It grows on trees and rocks, next to streams and ponds, and even on sidewalks. It is soft and fuzzy when wet, and brittle and scratchy when dry.

Find a piece of moss. If it is wet, take a small piece and put it in a dry place for a few days. When it has dried out, examine it through your hand lens. Does it look dead or alive? What color are the leaves and stems? Pour a little water on it and continue to view it through your lens. Can you see it expand like a sponge? Does the color change?

Lichens

On the shaded side of a tree you might find small cups and flattened growths of many colors: green, yellow, blue-green, orange and even red. These are called **lichens**, and they are as weird as they look. Besides being different colors, they come in different forms. Lichens can be thread-like, leafy, or crusty.

Search trees and boulders with your lens to see how many kinds of lichens you can find.

Lichens are composed of two different plants (**algae** and **fungi**) living together. Fungi come in many shapes and forms from athlete's foot to bread mold to toadstools. Algae can be found as pond scum or microscopic sea plants. Like other green plants, algae need sunlight, water and air to make food. They can't grow on dry places, such as rocks or tree trunks, without help. Fungi can't make their own food, but they can get water from the air.

Together fungi and algae can live almost anywhere because each provides the other with the things they need. The fungi get food from the algae and the algae get a moist home from the fungi.

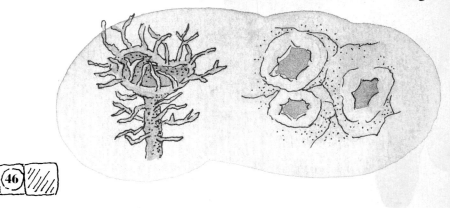

Scan the surface of a lichen and look for small trumpets or cups that appear as if they are filled with soup or jam.

These are called **ascocarps** and contain the seedlike parts (called **spores**) of the fungi. These spores get picked up by the wind and are carried here and there. If they land in a place where there is algae and moist air, a lichen may form.

The air is filled with fungal spores. In fact, this very instant you are probably breathing some in. Do you think you'll ever grow lichen in your nose?

How long does it take a lichen plant to grow?

Visit a cemetery and use your lens to look at lichens on the head-stones. Measure the lichens on different stones and compare the size to the age of the headstone.

PLANTS

Barking Up the Right Tree

You don't have to go to Arizona to see grand canyons and mysterious crevices. Just take a look at an old tree. As bark stretches, it breaks into long ropey ridges, rectangular plates or furrowed canyons. Some bark even sheds paper-thin strips or pieces that look like they came from a jigsaw puzzle.

Trees, like people, bleed when they are cut. Sap, the lifeblood of plants, hardens into pitch on the surface of the bark just like blood forms a scab on your skin. When this happens the bark gets sticky.

Stand belly up to a tree and take a visual hike with your lens. Imagine traveling across this strange landscape. Watch out for crevasses and sticky blobs of pitch. Beware of holes where insects and other animals have entered or exited from the tree.

A Real Flower House

What would it be like to live in a home where petals were your walls, floor and ceiling? That's what a thrip home looks like. **Thrips** are little insects, not much bigger that a freckle, that live, dine, and rest in flowers. You can find thrips by shaking flowers over a white piece of paper. You'll know thrips when you find them. They have feathery wings and often wiggle their tails.

Are you ready to see a thrip's living room? Grab your lens and peek into an open flower such as an apple blossom, buttercup, tulip or hollyhock. Knock, knock. Anyone home? See any thrips? Do you notice how the walls (petals) all come from the center of the flower? Look near the base where the petals join together and you will see some odd structures that may look like towers, urns, columns or tree branches.

Seed Factories

Flowers are seed factories and the strange structures inside are the production facilities. In the very center of the flower is a part called the **pistil**. Some flowers, such as strawberries, magnolias and buttercups, have a mound of pistils, while others like tulips have only one. At the top of the pistil is the **stigma** (a place where pollen can grow), and at the base is the **ovary** where the eggs rest inside.

STIGMA

PISTIL

OVARY

Did you know that when you take a bite of an apple you are munching on the swollen ovary of an apple blossom? It's true! When bees deposit pollen from other apple blossoms onto an apple blossom pistil, strange things begin to happen. The pollen starts to grow into the pistil and sends sperm (which fertilize the eggs) down to the ovary. Presto! A tiny apple with seeds begins to form. Within a few months, a full-grown apple hangs on the tree.

Take a look at the bottom of an apple. Can you find the shriveled stigma and other flower parts?

Pollen Pillows

Would you like to sleep on a soft flower pillow? If you were a thrip you could sleep on pillows packed with pollen. These pillows, called **anthers**, are the top parts of towers, called **stamens**. There are at least two stamens in each flower, and they grow in a circle around the pistil. As a flower matures the pillow (anther) pops open. When bees or other small flower guests bump into a ripe anther, they get a pollen shower. The pollen is then carried off to other flowers.

Look inside a flower for tall towers topped by pillows. Look at the anthers to see if any pollen is visible. What color is it? Pollen can be red, blue, orange or other colors.

Flower Condominiums

Flowers vary tremendously in shape, color and number of parts. The daisy is one of the most complex of flowers.

Peer through your lens at a daisy and you will notice that it is actually a combination of many tiny flowers. In the center of the daisy the flowers are RAY *shaped like funnels, and along the edges the flowers look like rays of the sun. Most people think that each ray is a petal. Take a close look and you will notice that each individual ray has a pistil, making it a flower in its own right. A daisy is a flower condominium.*

DISC

Secret Messages

Many flowers have secret messages written on their petals. A violet has stripes called **nectar guides** which show bees where to find the nectar inside the flower. Other flowers have bull's-eye patterns. These tell visitors to each flower that the nectar is at its center.

Look inside a variety of flowers for different patterns such as nectar guides and bull's-eyes. As you view them through your lens, pretend you are a bee coming in for a landing.

Hey, Bud

Have you ever eaten a flower?

Take a look at a head of broccoli. Check the top and you will notice many small green bumps. Peer at the bumps with your lens. Do you notice that each bump is a tiny bud?

Each bud has a set of small leaves, called **sepals**, which overlays the petals inside. Sometimes when broccoli is left in the refrigerator for too long, the sepals open and the broccoli blooms. Since the petals are yellow, the head starts to turn yellow, too.

Scat, Molds and Other Yucky Stuff

By this time you have probably used your lens to view some pretty weird stuff. Now you get to look at some really gross, terrible things. Why? Looking at gross stuff makes you tough. Your friends will think you are super bold (or maybe crazy). Looking at gross stuff also leads to great discoveries.

Take moldy old oranges for instance. Most people toss moldy old oranges away, but the blue-green mold is a source of a valuable medicine, an antibiotic called **penicillin**. Penicillin helps people fight diseases and would never have been discovered if people hadn't looked at mold.

Visit a friend who never cleans the refrigerator. Find a moldy orange and take a look for yourself. On a developing mold colony you will see fuzzy mats of white and blue-green hairs. These are the mold plants. Leave the orange around for a few days and you will notice little ping-pong balls on stilts. These are the fruiting bodies which produce the spores that grow into new mold colonies. Mold also grows on bread. Take a look at a moldy piece of bread. You can make your own by placing a slice in a plastic bag for a few days. Or simply look at that lunch you left in your desk last week! Does the bread mold look like the mold on an orange?

Take a Scatological Excursion

The next adventure will require even more guts. Are you ready to look at animal droppings (yeah, droppings are poop). Before you start, you can give poop a new name. Naturalists call mammal droppings **scat**, and insect droppings **frass**. Poop might not seem so bad if you call it by a new name.

Look for scat in an area where you might expect to see wild animals. It is often dropped along the trail, left on a rock or found at the entrance to an animal's burrow. Before you collect the scat make sure it is dry. Dry scat does not smell, and it doesn't look so gross either.

Looking at scat is one way to discover what animals eat. Find a lizard scat and you will discover tons of insect skins. A coyote or fox scat will reveal hairs, teeth, bones, and the skins and seeds of fruits. It's not uncommon to find a perfectly intact mouse jaw or a small claw. The scat of rabbits and squirrels doesn't contain much more than plant fiber, although occasionally you might find part of a bug. Porcupine droppings look like little "Presto Logs."

Insect frass comes in interesting shapes. Caterpillar frass can look like exotic beads, while that of others looks like miniature b-b's.

Reminder:
Wash your hands when you finish frassing around!!!

Lessons in Slow Motion

Has anyone ever said to you, "Hey, slow down!"? If you want to learn about slow motion take lessons from an earthworm. Worms never run or skip about. They move like slinkies or long accordions as they slither over and through the ground. Worms hide out in tunnels in the soil, and you can track them down by looking for their castings. **Castings** are the plaster that worms use to cover the walls of their burrows. They are a mixture of mucus and soil that is swirled out like soft ice cream. Excess castings are dumped at the mouth of worm burrows.

Look for some castings on a lawn or in a garden. Examine them with your lens and then dig a hole beneath them. When you find an earthworm, place it on a piece of moist paper toweling and survey it with your lens. Return it to its home when you are done.

Since earthworms don't wear hats, it's hard at first to tell which end the head is on. Like most animals, worms travel head first. As your worm moves, notice how it swings its head around and pokes and prods with its snout-like upper lip called its **prostonium**. Using its prostonium like a grappling hook, a worm pulls itself along and snags leaves and other food. Worms also have pairs of short stiff hairs, called **setae**, which work like soccer cleats to help them get a grip on difficult terrain.

Glance at the worm from the side with the lens and you may notice pairs of setae or bristles on the its undersection. The setae are easy to see when a worm is rolled on its back.

A worm wears more rings than a movie star. In fact, the entire length of the body is made of muscular rings. Worms move by stretching and contracting these rings.

With your lens examine the rings as the worm moves. Do you notice how they get wider and narrower? Touch your worm and watch how it pulls itself in. Below the head you may notice a large ring, called the saddle or **clitellum**. The saddle is only found on adults and is used to help make baby worms.

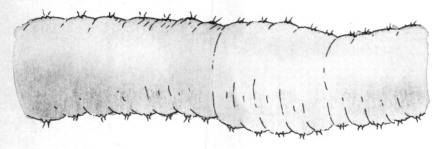

Experiment with your worm. Watch what it does when it comes to an obstacle or a pool of water. Will it go over or under a leaf? Place a worm on some loose soil and watch it burrow. How long does it take to go under?

A Gastropod's Pace

If you are ready to take an even slower journey, find a slug or snail. You've surely heard someone say, "You move at a snail's pace" or "what a slug!" These slimy creatures are constantly put down by people who don't appreciate their lack of speed, but snails survive perfectly well without living in the fast lane. They are easy to find because they always leave behind a silvery trail of slime. As they glide over rugged surfaces they ooze slime to help make it a smooth cruise.

Look for snails or slugs under damp logs, old boards or the leaves of garden plants. Collect one and set it on a piece of paper. Examine it with your lens.

Bigfoot

Snails and slugs have neither arms nor legs; instead, they possess one big foot. This muscular foot doesn't get them anywhere at high speed, but it does get them from place to place (eventually).

Put a snail or slug on a clear plastic container lid. Using the lens, watch it glide. Do you notice how the foot pulses like a wave? What does it look like from underneath?

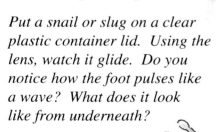

YUCKY

Eye to Eye

Snails and slugs look like smooth-skinned creatures, but up close they are as wrinkled as elephants. Unlike elephants, they have two sets of feelers. One set helps them feel and smell their neighborhood. The other is topped with a pair of eyes. Both sets retract, like the radio antennae on a sports car, when snails or slugs sense danger. Snails and slugs are the only animals with heads on their feet. That is why they are called **gastropods**, which is Latin for "mouth feet."

Get eye to eye with a gastropod. Peer through the lens at the end of the long set of feelers. Can you see the eyes on the end? These small black eyes can't see you clearly, but they can sense light and dark. What happens when you touch the feelers? Give the slug or snail a leaf to eat. Does it scrape the leaf with its mouth?

Slime Time

Snails and slugs depend on slime for their survival. The shells which protect snails from enemies form layer by layer from crystals of calcium that ooze out of a body part called the **mantle**. Slugs also have a mantle, but their shell consists only of a few crystals hidden under the skin.

YUCKY

Slime also keeps their skin moist, and without this ooze they cannot cruise. Imagine if you had to rely on slime for your transportation.

Examine a snail shell with your lens. Can you see the layers? Look closely at the back section of the mantle of a slug. You might get to see it squirting out slime. Don't let it slime you! Be sure to place your snail or slug back in its slimy home when you're done.

S' not Funny

Slime is pretty serious stuff. Without the slimy mucus that coats our breathing apparatus (mouth, nose, throat and lungs) we would be goners.

Mucus protects us from most of the dangerous things floating about in the air. It traps dust and germs that we breathe in, but allows air and water to pass through.

Be bold! Look at some mucus. Get some by blowing your nose or coughing up some phlegm. Check it out with your lens and remember to wash your hands when you're done. (You wouldn't want anything to stick to them!)

The End?

This is almost the end of the book, but it shouldn't be the end of your explorations of the World of Small. Wild, exotic sights are hidden all around you. Be bold, curious, adventuresome! Make amazing discoveries in your own back yard (or anywhere else you visit).

You can follow the example of other intrepid travelers:

Delhia Gomez of Cuba City, Wisconsin, *found that egg shells have little pits on the outside.*

Elvis Birdwell of Dull Center, Wyoming, *amazed his friends and family when he showed them a close-up view of a sharpened pencil.*

Ruthie Duxbury of Los Angeles, California, *was intrigued by the magnified view of her grandmother's eyeshadow.*

Jimmy Zizzo of Massapequa, New York, *spent days peering into his brother's ear.*

Take your lens with you wherever you go. Who knows what weird and fascinating sights await you?

Now, if you want to find out about the history of lenses, check out the next page.

A Short History of Magnification

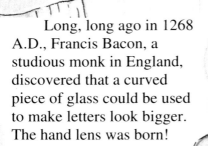

A long, long, long time ago before people kept time, Martha, one of the ancient people, noticed that things looked bigger in water.

Long, long, long ago in 63 B.C., Seneca, a Roman philosopher, described how to fill a glass globe with water and look through it to make things appear bigger.

Long, long ago in 1268 A.D., Francis Bacon, a studious monk in England, discovered that a curved piece of glass could be used to make letters look bigger. The hand lens was born!

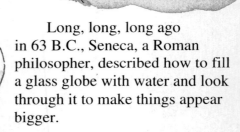